*The Transformation
of Western
Pennsylvania
1770–1800*

The Transformation
of Western
Pennsylvania
1770–1800

R. Eugene Harper

University of Pittsburgh Press

F
153
H37
1991

Published by the University of Pittsburgh Press, Pittsburgh, PA 15260
Copyright © 1991, University of Pittsburgh Press

Eurospan, London

Manufactured in the United States of America

Library of Congress Cataloging-in-Publication Data

Harper, R. Eugene.
    The transformation of Western Pennsylvania, 1770–1800 / R. Eugene
Harper.
        p. cm.
    Includes bibliographical references and index.
    ISBN 0-8229-3678-X
    1. Pennsylvania—History—1775–1865. 2. Social classes—
Pennsylvania—History—18th century. 3. Pennsylvania—Social
conditions. 4. Pennsylvania—Economic conditions. I. Title.
F153.H37   1991
974.8'803—dc20   90-28574
                                                          CIP

A CIP Catalogue Record for this book is available from the British Library.

To My Parents
Robert M. and Martha B. Harper

Contents

Preface

STANDING ON the bluff of Friendship Hill, gazing down at the Monongahela River and the hills in the distance, one enters a world two centuries past. Would Albert Gallatin recognize this view from his homestead? Surely the river, with its constant pool of water and many evidences of industry and mining, would be shocking, but above the river itself, the wooded hills probably look much as they did when Gallatin and his new wife, Sophia, came here in 1789.

I first visited Friendship Hill years ago when it served as the destination for grade school field trips. Next to Fort Necessity in the mountains at Great Meadows, where George Washington touched off the French and Indian War, Friendship Hill was the favorite school trip. Later the estate fell into disrepair and was boarded up. Fortunately, it is now undergoing full restoration by the National Park Service. Little could I have known in those grade school years that I would return many years later to roam the grounds and sense its ambiance because I had undertaken to study the history of early western Pennsylvania.

Then there is the Isaac Meason plantation. Every Sunday my family would drive past it on the way to visit my grandparents. The sandstone Georgian mansion stood majestically in its open fields, a landmark, but little appreciated by most passersby. Today it is listed on the National Register of Historic Places, but the grounds and house are threatened by proposed strip mining. Gazing at the house, one can hardly imagine the activity that must have engulfed it two centuries ago when it served as the center of a bustling iron plantation.

To study the history of one's home region is to embark upon a project with many rewards. The subject matter is endlessly interesting and fascinating. The data constantly reveal information about things familiar and provide an appreciation and a deeper understanding of their origins. One drives along local highways with a new sense of awareness, gazes across the landscape to picture yeoman farmsteads in early stages of development, stops at local sites to ponder the lives and events of the past, and turns down unknown lanes to explore newly discovered places.

As a graduate student at the University of Pittsburgh, I first began to explore local history. A seminar paper led to a master's thesis, and later the thesis led to a Ph.D. dissertation. Now comes this book. The path between those events has not been straight; deviations have occurred and years have intervened. Only gradually has the history of the region taken on an interpretive framework that pulls together the people and events of the past into an integrated whole.

Standing at Friendship Hill or looking at Meason's plantation, one is struck by how rapidly western Pennsylvania was transformed from a wilderness into a thriving society. When Albert and Sophia Gallatin set foot on Friendship Hill, it was only thirty-five years after George Washington had engaged the French at Fort Necessity. Initially, Friendship Hill was just a crude home on the edge of the frontier. Sophia died within the year. Yet, within a half-dozen years, Gallatin had turned his estate into a manufacturing center for glass, guns, and boats. Isaac Meason also transformed his farm into a manufacturing center, employing 10 percent of the township's population in the 1790s.

Between the 1780s and the end of the century, western Pennsylvania turned from a crude frontier region into a functioning society. The degree of transformation, of course, was relative and varied from place to place. But the evidence of rapid change was everywhere: in the pattern of land-ownership, in the rise of towns, in the occupational structure, in the development of commercial agriculture, in the political institutions. Alexander Addison summarized his sense of this rapid change in September 1794. Addison, president judge of the

Fifth Judicial Circuit of Pennsylvania, in his famous charge to the grand jury during the Whiskey Rebellion, stated:

> The progess of this country to wealth has been amazingly rapid. Three years ago, there was hardly a burr millstone in this country: now there are perhaps a dozen. The quantity of money circulating among us is since greatly increased; and the value of all property is thereby greatly increased; in other words, the value of money is greatly lessened, and thereby the value of the excise to be paid by us is greatly lessened. Then there was hardly any trade to the Spanish settlements on the Mississippi; it was, at any rate, small and confined to a few adventurers: The quantity of grain exported was but little; of course but little was withdrawn from our own consumption; and this little was generally bought with goods.
>
> Now a very respectable trade is carried on to the Spanish settlements; our traders are treated with great civility by the Spaniards; the duty on our trade is reduced to a mere trifle and there is very little difficulty in bringing away dollars in return. We shall soon have the whole supply of that market to ourselves. Last spring, our best flour sold there a dollar each barrel dearer than flour from New York.—None of the traders now depend on goods for the purchase of wheat; but must purchase, at a reasonable price, in money.[1]

Addison, of course, was making a partisan appeal to his countrymen to end their rebellion. He sought to show them that it was to their economic advantage to do so. Nevertheless, his words give evidence of the changes under way in western Pennsylvania. It is the fundamental conclusion of this study that Judge Addison was correct in his claim that progress was "amazingly rapid."

While publication of this work adds to the growing literature of early community studies, it has benefited greatly from the recent scholarship that makes clear many of the social and economic relationships of early America. These studies have, in various ways, illustrated the gradual stages of transformation from traditional to modern society, the complexity of relationships, and the maturing of economies that this transformation involved. Those transformations and complexities in western Pennsylvania, however, were condensed into a single generation.

When the earliest research for this study was begun, historians were debating the merits of revisionist historical works that sought to modify the Beardian-Progressive interpretation of American history. In particular, they searched for signs of local democracy to counteract the Progressive view that early America was dominated by a wealthy elite acting for its own benefit. Robert and Katherine Brown were particularly active in seeking a "middle class" democracy in early America, but others such as Merle Curti and Charles Grant also sought democracy by studying early communities.[2]

Another source for local history study came from the concerns of New Left historians who, in the 1960s and 1970s, argued that history ought to be studied "from the bottom up." They were joined by labor and social historians who also sought to understand the history of the common people— those on the "underside" of society. Jesse Lemish led this movement with his study of seamen in the Revolution, and Robert Young told the story of a craftsman of the same period. Labor and social historians have added a number of studies on the working class in early America.[3]

The most significant source for recent studies of local communities, however, has come from the new social historians. Motivated by a concern for the structures of society as well as an interest in the common people, and informed by social science research methods and computer capabilities, they have turned out local studies that have revolutionized our understanding of early American society. These vary widely, from studies of population and family to a search for community; from analysis of local and regional economic systems to political and even psychological analysis.

Community studies came into their own in 1970 with the publication of five works now considered standards and widely cited in bibliographies of early American history. The way had been shown by Charles Grant's study that dealt with society as much as with democracy, and by Sumner Powell and Darrett Rutman; but the work on Massachusetts towns by Philip Greven (Andover), Kenneth Lockridge (Dedham), and

John Demos (Plymouth) called widespread attention to and provided models for local community studies. They were joined by Richard Bushman's study of Connecticut and Michael Zuckerman's study of New England towns.[4] The New England town was particularly well suited for detailed study because of its size and continuity. As a result, many other New England communities have been the subjects of dissertations and monographs as varied as Robert Zemsky's on the Connecticut River Valley, Robert Gross's on Concord, and Paul Boyer and Stephen Nissenbaum's on Salem.[5]

The Chesapeake area was not left out of these community studies. Led by the work of Aubrey Land, many studies have focused on early Maryland. Among them, Russell Menard and Paul Clemens have analyzed the economic system, and Lois Green Carr, Lorena Walsh, and others have produced a wealth of data on local living standards.[6] Important studies of Virginia include those by Richard Beeman and by Darrett and Anita Rutman as well broader reconsiderations of Virginia by Allan Kulikoff and Rhys Isaac.[7]

Colonial cities have also received their share of analysis. Beginning with James Henretta's study of Boston, which shows the consolidation of wealth and power that occurred throughout the eighteenth century, Gary Nash, Billy G. Smith, Allan Kulikoff, G. B. Warden, and others have produced many works delving into the life and work of colonial urban dwellers.[8] All of these community studies owe much to the pioneering work of Jackson Main, who produced the standard description of early American social structure, and whose work is still the baseline from which most studies proceed.[9]

Pennsylvania, of course, has not been ignored. The equivalent of the Jackson Main work for Pennsylvania is the classic study of southeastern Pennsylvania by James Lemon. His work on Chester and Lancaster counties in the eighteenth century provides baselines for all American historians on how early agricultural communities functioned. Also well received have been Stephanie Wolf's study of Germantown and Jerome Wood's study of Lancaster. These works have been very helpful to this study.[10]

These local community studies have deepened our understanding of the social relationships of early American society. The search for a middle-class democracy had the ironic result of focusing attention on the widespread existence of land-lessness and tenancy. The well-known tenancy of the Hudson River Valley received definitive treatment by Sung Bok Kim, but tenancy has also been studied in New England, the Chesapeake region, and Pennsylvania. Lucy Simler's studies of tenancy in Chester County have been particularly relevant to an understanding of western Pennsylvania.[11]

The more recent local histories have shown how common people actually supported themselves. Self-sufficiency studies have defined intricate systems of local exchange, renting, and mutual obligation that have enriched our understanding. Again, the work of Paul Clemens and Lucy Simler has been particularly helpful in understanding what was occurring in western Pennsylvania during the late 1700s.[12]

Much of the original research for this study of the social history of western Pennsylvania was begun at the time Philip Greven, Kenneth Lockridge, and John Demos were preparing their work on New England towns. In its dissertation form, this study provided a basis for two important studies of the Whiskey Rebellion, western Pennsylvania's pivotal event.[13] After the University of Pittsburgh Press agreed to publish this work, many revisions were made to take advantage of recent scholarship, but the essential data base remains unchanged.

This study has both temporal and geographical limits. The time period involved is primarily the 1780s and 1790s. Settlement was officially allowed in the region following the Fort Stanwix Treaty of 1768, and the first county government was established in 1773 when Westmoreland County was erected. Unfortunately, few local records are available prior to the 1780s. A terminal date of 1796 was chosen for this study because I was then able to avoid a number of logistical problems. For example, all Greene County data prior to that date would be found in Washington County, since the former was carved out of the latter. It also avoids the problems caused by the mass creation of eight new northwestern counties in 1800. By including 1796, however, I could use several new items—

especially occupations—that appear on the assessments for the first time that year following changes in the tax laws in 1795. For these reasons, the years involved in the study are primarily 1783 through 1796, but some specific references do extend to either side of these dates.

Geographically, the study focuses upon southwestern Pennsylvania, particularly the Monongahela River basin. The area includes the five present-day counties of Allegheny, Fayette, Greene, Washington, and Westmoreland. All of these counties lie wholly or partially west of the mountains and constitute a natural geographic entity.

The primary data exploited in this study are the records available in the courthouses of the various counties. The dockets and minute books of the courts of Quarter Sessions, Quarter Sessions papers, and the dockets and papers of the courts of Common Pleas for all the counties have been used. Some use has been made of deed books and other extant early records. The most important local sources, however, were the tax assessment records of the various counties. These local records have been supplemented by information published in the *Pennsylvania Archives,* by state statutes, several county histories, and studies of county government.

The specific tax assessments used in this study were chosen on the basis of completeness, comparable intervals of time, and the fullest possible geographical coverage. Thus, the assessments chosen for detailed study were those for Westmoreland County in 1783, Washington County in 1784—both found in the *Pennsylvania Archives*—and Fayette County in 1785. These provided full coverage of the entire region in the mid-1780s. The assessments selected for the 1790s were those from Washington County in 1793 and Fayette County in 1796. These assessments covered only half of the region, since there are no local tax records for Allegheny and Westmoreland counties in the 1790s, but they allowed comparisons with Washington and Fayette counties at approximately one-decade intervals.

The fundamental question that must be answered with regard to the sources used for this study is simply: How valid are tax assessments for studying the class structure of western

Pennsylvania? Are wills and inventories a more valuable source?[14] Insofar as western Pennsylvania in the late eighteenth century is concerned, assessments are the better source for several reasons. First, people who make wills are more likely to be people with estates to dispose of rather than people with little or no property.[15] In a society as new and transient as western Pennsylvania was during the first generation, wills would likely give a misleading picture. This was a society in which 60 percent of the males were under twenty-one years of age. Very few would have accumulated significant estates from their work in the local economy, but many probably brought wealth with them when they came to the area.

It is also doubtful that, during this first generation, a representative number of people would have yet died. For example, the first will book for Allegheny County includes less than a seventh of the taxable males shown on the 1790 census.[16] By comparison, assessments—as will be shown later—covered approximately 90 percent of the taxable males. Wills and inventories do add depth and dimension to any outline of the class structure, and in matters of nontaxable wealth such as merchant inventories, investments, and personal property, wills are superior to tax data. Over longer periods of time, wills and inventories do illustrate changing patterns of social wealth and consumption. Nevertheless, because of the newness of the area, and in order to measure as wide a cross section of the population as possible by a single standard, tax assessments have been used for this study.

This question then remains—How wide a cross section of the population is included in the tax assessments? If a significant number of males of taxable age do not appear on the tax lists, then tax lists are not much better than wills. However, several factors promoted relatively complete lists. First, Pennsylvania's tax laws placed a head tax on each single freeman— that is, a single male, aged twenty-one and above—whether he had taxable property or not. Thus, these young persons, who would otherwise have been missed, appeared on the tax lists.[17] Second, the tax law of 1795, which became effective for the assessments of 1796, laid a specific tax on each occupation. Thus, even the poorest artisan could not escape taxation at that point.[18] In addition, the fact that the area was newly settled meant that there would be a smaller indigent population than would be found in older, more urban areas. This secondary evidence, therefore, suggests that there should not have been any large, unknown body of propertyless persons in western Pennsylvania in the late eighteenth century. Comparisons of tax lists with the taxable population confirm the fact that tax lists represent approximately 90 percent of the taxable male population.

These figures have been derived by comparing lists of taxable persons with the censuses of 1790 and 1800. Although the 1790 census did not include a population subdivision at age twenty-one, it is possible, by beginning with the population breakdowns of the 1800 census and projecting percentages backward, to estimate the number of males aged twenty-one and above in 1790 and in the 1780s.[19] Two important figures emerge from studying the 1800 census. First, the percentage of males who were aged twenty-one and above was 39.4 percent of the total male population. Second, the percentage of males aged sixteen to twenty-one, a figure necessary for studying the 1790 census, was 9.1 percent of the total males. Preface table 1 depicts the relationship between those

PREFACE TABLE 1
The Relationship Between Taxable Population and Tax Lists by County,
Western Pennsylvania, 1800

County	Taxable Population (males 21 years and older)	Taxable Population on Tax Lists	
		Number	Percentage
Westmoreland	4,537	4,404	97.1
Washington	5,782	5,094	88.1
Fayette	4,051	3,779	93.3
Allegheny	3,051	2,501	82.0
Greene	1,684	1,576	93.6
Total	19,105	17,354	90.8

Source: Population figures were taken from the *Second U.S. Census, 1800.* A full list of taxable persons for Pennsylvania at seven-year intervals may be found in Samuel Hazard, ed., *Hazard's Register of Pennsylvania* (Philadelphia, 1828–1835), 4 (July 1829), pp. 12–13.

taxed and the potential taxable population in 1800; approximately 90 percent of the taxable population of 1800 was represented by the tax lists of that year.

In the 1790 census, for which only one age subdivision was given, there were 15,401 males aged sixteen and older in western Pennsylvania. By subtracting 9.1 percent of the total males, representing those aged sixteen to twenty-one as derived from the 1800 census, there remained 12,380 males aged twenty-one and over who were eligible to be taxed. The numbers of taxables given by *Hazard's Register* for the counties of Western Pennsylvania in 1786 and 1793 were 8,602 and 13,850, respectively. In 1790, on the basis of a direct, proportional increase, western Pennsylvania should have had a taxable population of approximately 11,602 persons.[20] Therefore, approximately 94 percent of the taxable population of 12,380 would have been represented by the 11,602 persons calculated for the tax lists. (Computing an estimated population for 1793 and comparing that with the 1793 taxables gave a similar 94 percent representation.)

When dealing with the period of the 1780s, there is no census to act as a guide, and the total population is estimated at 33,500.[21] However, by taking the projection of males in the free populations of 1800 and 1790 and projecting this back into the 1780s, it has been estimated that 54 percent of the population of 1783–1784 were males. If approximately 40 percent of them were taxable males, then there were some 7,236 males aged twenty-one and above in 1783–1784 who were eligible to be taxed. The tax assessments for Westmoreland and Washington counties in those years contained 7,204 taxables.[22]

On the basis of these comparisons, there can be little doubt that the tax data of the late eighteenth century is a valid means for analyzing the class structure of western Pennsylvania at that time. During the 1780s, when western Pennsylvania was a new frontier, the projected correlation between taxables and males of taxable age is almost exact. As time passed, the correlation becomes less exact, but even in 1800, it is still approximately 90 percent. There are certain other factors to take into consideration. Absentee landowners appear on many township assessments, as do a few women who were heads of families. Such people obviously inflated the assessment figures. On the other hand, some of the propertyless population undoubtedly escaped detection. Even admitting these difficulties—and they may cancel each other—for the years of this study, there can be little doubt that tax assessments do represent the vast majority of the population of western Pennsylvania.

A final word should be added regarding money. Until 1796, all monetary values used on the assessments were in English pounds: twelve pennies to the shilling and twenty shillings to the pound. On the 1796 assessments for Fayette County, dollars were used for the first time. The conversion rate widely used in the region was £3=$8. Values given in the text are those of the original document whether pounds or dollars.

The preparation of any historical work owes so much to so many people that they all cannot be singled out. To the many friendly and dedicated people who work in the local courthouses, especially in Fayette, Washington, and Westmoreland counties, I owe a special debt. They provided records, dug out items rarely used, answered many questions, and provided work space day after day for that odd young man who poured over their materials during graduate school days; they continue to render the same caring services years later. I am comforted to find that there has been significant improvement in the care with which local records are kept, but the pressures confronting local governments faced with expanding records, limited storage space, and meager resources continue to pose very real problems. Charles Stock, librarian of the Washington County Law Library, into whose care the original assessment records are now entrusted, rather than stored under the courthouse roof as they once were, is due special commendation for his care and helpfulness. To the others—officials, clerks, secretaries, custodians—thank you.

The librarians of several institutions provided access to their collections with unfailing skill and courtesy: the Darlington Room and the Hillman Library of the University of Pittsburgh, the Pennsylvania Room of the Carnegie Library of

Pittsburgh, the Western Pennsylvania Historical Society, Washington and Jefferson College, the public libraries in Uniontown and Washington, and the West Virginia Archives.

One is always in debt to one's teachers. Emory Evans and Samuel Hays deserve credit for early influences at the University of Pittsburgh. Van Beck Hall has been a true mentor and friend over the years. Dorothy Fennell, whose excellent dissertation on the Whiskey Rebellion used some of the individual data developed for this study, added her encouragement. A special debt of gratitude is due Treasa Russell, who transferred the dissertation text to computer disks for subsequent revision. Frederick A. Hetzel and Catherine Marshall of the University of Pittsburgh Press have been most cooperative and helpful in bringing this book to press.

To Susan, Heather, Glenn, and Seth, my wife and children, I owe a special thank you. Each of them contributed in some way to this work, from copying original records in the courthouse to editing and proofreading. They all bore the publication process with good cheer. Finally, to my parents, who were born and lived their lives in Fayette County, and who gave me many reasons to appreciate my home, this book is gratefully dedicated.

*The Transformation
of Western
Pennsylvania
1770–1800*

1 Early Settlement: Problems and Promises

THE TRANSFORMATION of the western Pennsylvania frontier began in conflict and instability yet proceeded rapidly throughout the late eighteenth century in spite of continuing problems. As was true of frontier regions in general, the advance of frontier society occurred at the expense of native Indian populations. The strategic location of the western Pennsylvania frontier guaranteed that these conflicts would be an early and continuing problem even into the 1790s.

> A party of Indians appeared at this place about noon to-day and intercepted an escourt of provisions, etc., which was bound to Lieu. Gray's Station. I was at the Mills when the men were receiving these stores, and left it about the same time they did, and before I reached my house, heard a few guns fired in quick succession near that place.

The writer of this extract from a 17 April 1792 letter to the militia lieutenant of Washington County was Thomas Ryerson, one of the county's wealthiest citizens. Ryerson had been a merchant in Philadelphia and had come to western Pennsylvania in the late 1780s. Most of the good land had been taken by then, so he purchased a 400-acre tract on the headwaters of Wheeling Creek in Finley Township on the western border of the county. Ryerson established both a sawmill and a gristmill on his land, and he engaged in land speculation on a vast scale—the largest in the county. Located only a few miles from the Ohio River, Ryerson's land was not difficult for Indian bands to reach.[1]

Such conflict was not unexpected in the 1790s due to the warfare in Ohio. Lawyer David Redick had written the Pennsylvania governor, Thomas Mifflin, in February 1792 that "a considerable gap is left open to the enemy on the North westerly part of the County," a direction from which attack had frequently come in past conflicts. The previous year, Congressman William Findley of Westmoreland County reported to the secretary of the commonwealth, A. J. Dallas, in April 1791, that he was "informed that a blockhouse opposite to Pittsburgh" had been attacked, but the opponents were repulsed. He reported again in June 1792 that raids had taken place in northern Westmoreland County. The continuing military crisis on the frontier produced many such reports from western Pennsylvania officials.[2]

By the 1790s, however, Indian conflicts were normally limited to the remote frontier regions and involved only occasional raids by small roving bands. The real conflict had now been transferred to Ohio. Ryerson notes this new reality in his letter when he suggested to the county lieutenant that a few militia should be sent to the area in order to keep conflict "at as great a distance from the populous settlements as possible."[3] Nevertheless, because the frontier transformation had taken so little time, memories of Dunmore's War, a conflict with the Shawnee Indians in the 1770s, and the Revolution were fresh in the minds of many settlers, and the revived warfare of the 1790s in Ohio was unsettling.

If clashes with Indians were the most dramatic conflict, they were not the only one experienced by settlers in western Pennsylvania. The immigration patterns brought into the region two groups of people who had different ethnic backgrounds and loyalties. Both Pennsylvania and Virginia claimed western Pennsylvania, and the resulting clash of loyalties led to a number of bitter confrontations and complications before the two states settled their boundary dispute. The revolutionary war placed additional heavy military strains on the region's limited manpower and agricultural production, already stretched to protect the region from British-inspired Indian attacks.

Nevertheless, settlers continued to enter the region even during the Revolution. Following the war, the rate of population growth accelerated, peaked in the early 1790s, and then slowed to approximately the same rate of increase as for the state as a whole by the end of the century. Before the Revolution, western Pennsylvania had many characteristics of a new frontier. The population surge after the war, however, speeded the transformation into a stable society. The slowing of this population surge coincided with many indicators of societal maturity and marked the end of the frontier period. The difficulties experienced during the first years of settlement form the background for this study, but the accomplishments of this period of transformation are its primary concern.

The Geographical Pattern of Settlement

As settlers streamed into western Pennsylvania, the Monongahela River valley provided the geographical focal point of settlement. The river divides what became Fayette and Westmoreland counties on the east from the future Washington and Greene counties on the west. The eastern half of Fayette and Westmoreland counties also contain the last ridges of the Appalachian Mountains, before the topography gives way to the rolling foothills that dominate the rest of the region. Into this river valley, and the lands adjacent to its tributary streams, came settlers from two directions. One stream of settlers came from eastern Pennsylvania and New Jersey, following the military road cut by Gen. John Forbes. They entered western Pennsylvania from the northeast and spread toward the southwest over Westmoreland, northern Fayette, and eastern Allegheny counties. These people had the greater ethnic diversity associated with the middle colonies, and they brought strong Pennsylvania loyalties with them. A second stream of immigrants, from Maryland and Virginia, came from the southeast on the military road cut by Gen. Edward Braddock. These settlers entered more directly into the Monongahela valley, and gave to Washington and Greene counties, to southern Allegheny County, and to parts of Fayette County a more homogeneous English population with stronger Virginia loyalties.[4]

The exact ethnic composition of the settlers, however, is very unclear. For a half-century, the question of ethnicity seemed answered. Historians widely accepted the distinctive surname methodology for determining ethnicity developed by Howard F. Barker in 1931. Using that methodology, Solon Buck concluded that an English-Welsh group was in the majority in Washington, Fayette, and Allegheny counties, the three counties with the greatest number of settlers from Maryland and Virginia.[5] According to Barker, in both Maryland and Virginia, the English-Welsh group comprised more than 60 percent of the population, and some of this same predominance was carried over into these three counties of western Pennsylvania, in Buck's calculations. A Calvinist group of Irish and Scottish settlers comprised the second largest cultural group in the region and the largest group in Westmoreland County. The German population was a distant third compared with the other two cultural groups but was twice as large in Fayette and Westmoreland as elsewhere. The greater diversity found in Westmoreland County reflected the ethnic composition of Pennsylvania, where Barker found the English and German populations about equal in size and where more ethnic groups appeared than in either Maryland or Virginia.[6]

Since 1980, however, Barker's methodology has come under rather devastating attack. On the one hand, some scholars find the underlying assumptions and tenuous methodologies so flawed as to reject the whole surname methodology. Others acknowledge specific criticisms of Barker's results but fundamentally accept the methods and have tried to refine them. The two most comprehensive revisions of Barker, those by Forrest McDonald and Ellen Shapiro McDonald and by Thomas Purvis, however, do not agree fully on a new set of numbers, especially for the vital area of English and Celtic immigration.[7]

One can achieve a rough consensus by averaging the differences in the two studies on the state level, but western Pennsylvania was settled by streams of migration from two states, each with very different ethnic compositions. How these two streams merged in western Pennsylvania can be only guessed until there is agreement on the precise methodology to be used, and until someone then tests the western Pennsylvania population directly. Thus, we know the standard figures are wrong, and the new figures should probably increase the German composition some, increase the Celtic composition more (and include the Welsh with the other Celts, not with the English), and reduce the English component. One example of the differences to be reconciled can be seen from the old standard figures that gave Washington County a Celtic composition of 45 percent, while the new estimates of the McDonalds suggest a Celtic composition for Washington County of over 75 percent.[8]

As these two waves of settlement entered western Pennsylvania, settlers generally bypassed the mountains and moved toward the river. This meant that in Fayette, Washington, and Greene counties, in particular, those townships located on the river and major tributary streams received much of the early settlement, while townships in the interior regions of these counties received secondary amounts of population. Both the mountainous east and the extreme western border regions of Washington and Greene counties were little touched by the earliest settlements. In Westmoreland County, where the geographical position was more distant from the Monongahela, settlement tended to be heaviest along and to the south of Forbes Road once it passed beyond the mountains, and also along the rivers in that part of Westmoreland that later become part of Allegheny County. The major exceptions to this pattern are the county seat townships located in the interior regions. Thus, the pattern of settlement had a definite geographical basis. It was most dense along the Monongahela River valley and became more sparse as it moved east and west from this central valley. In Westmoreland County, the pattern was more dense in the southwest and less dense on the north and east. In these river and advanced interior townships, the transformation of western Pennsylvania took place most rapidly. (The maps in appendix B will be helpful in clarifying this geographical pattern.)

Problems of Settlement

This geographical pattern of settlement was one of the important factors behind a number of problems that affected the first generation in western Pennsylvania. Much of the heat caused by the boundary dispute between Pennsylvania and Virginia was due to the two streams of migration that brought settlers with conflicting loyalties into the region. The dispute began in earnest when, in 1769, following the Fort Stanwix Treaty, Pennsylvania started to sell lands in the west that Virginia had long claimed and had defended during the French and Indian War. Matters came to a head when the English evacuated Fort Pitt and the earl of Dunmore was appointed governor of Virginia in 1772. Pennsylvania then established Westmoreland County in 1773, bringing Pennsylvania's jurisdiction beyond the mountains for the first time. Virginia countered by erecting the district of West Augusta in 1774 and then creating three counties out of West Augusta in 1776. These rival governments operated in the area from 1776 until 1780. On occasion, this rivalry blocked cooperation during the revolutionary war effort, and it added to the discontent expressed in the abortive new state movements in the region. In this nebulous situation, local officials found it difficult to perform their duties and to collect their legitimate share of taxes. When a final settlement of the dispute was achieved in 1780, it left a large body of disaffected persons under Pennsylvania jurisdiction. Many of them, including some slave owners who objected to Pennsylvania's Gradual Abolition Law of 1780, joined the Kentucky migrations. Others, however, including some important leaders, stayed and became reconciled to Pennsylvania jurisdiction.[9]

Closely connected to the divided governments and rival loyalties of the boundary dispute were the problems created by two competing land systems and a series of overlapping land grants. In brief, the Virginia system was more lenient, allowed larger holdings, and cost settlers less money. Until the Revolution, the government of colonial Virginia had taken no specific action with regard to land titles on its western borders. The colony's headright system of land grants and government grants to individuals had formed the basis for Virginia land claims in Pennsylvania and elsewhere. Once the royal government ended, the validity of these claims became doubtful. Recognizing this hazy state of affairs as well as the possible loss of western Pennsylvania and the need to protect its settlers there, Virginia passed two laws in 1779 establishing a system for settling western land titles and opening a land office. By terms of this Virginia law, 400 acres were granted to each family who were bona fide settlers as of 1 January 1778. Those persons who had had a survey anytime after 26 October 1763 for less than 400 acres were entitled to additional vacant lands to complete a 400-acre tract. Provision was also made for persons desiring larger tracts up to 1,000 acres, and the price of land was fixed at ten shillings per 100 acres. The law provided for commissioners to hear and adjust conflicting claims. These Virginia commissioners granted "scores of certificates" to Virginia claimants, 1,182 of which, totaling 634,371 acres, Pennsylvania later accepted as valid claims.[10]

By contrast, Pennsylvania had, by 1765, a definite application system for patenting vacant lands. When western Pennsylvania was officially opened for settlement in 1769, following purchase from the Indians the preceding year, this system was used to establish Pennsylvania titles. Under the system, a 300-acre tract was the largest that could be claimed by any one person, and no provision was made for larger grants. However, this provision could be circumvented by applying for lands in another person's name—a relative or business associate, perhaps—and then merely endorsing the true applicant's name on the back of the application. Speculators had no trouble getting large tracts. The Pennsylvania system, however, allowed only twelve-months' credit and required full payment before a patent would issue. The cost of land was fixed at £5 per 100 acres—ten times the Virginia rate—plus one penny per acre quit rent. The Revolution naturally closed the proprietary land office, and no office was reopened until 1781, after the boundary dispute had been settled, and then only to complete titles begun before the war. It was not until 1 July 1784 that the Pennsylvania land office again went into full operation, granting title to vacant lands under essentially the same old proprietary system. However, the 1784 law reduced the price of land in southwestern Pennsylvania to £3.10

per 100 acres and allowed 400-acre tracts as the maximum size. In 1792, the price of land was further lowered to £2.10. All quit rents were abolished with the Divesting Act of 1779.[11]

These competing land systems not only resulted in Pennsylvania accepting nearly 1,200 Virginia certificates as valid Pennsylvania titles, but the two systems were clearly reflected in the patterns of landownership of the 1780s. Washington County, the heart of Virginia sentiment, exhibited an ownership pattern built around the 400-acre grant, while Westmoreland County, the stronghold of Pennsylvania sentiment, had a pattern based upon the 300-acre grant.[12] Furthermore, it has been suggested that the more liberal Virginia land system had an adverse effect upon Westmoreland settlement. Settlers, presumably induced by the cheaper prices, tended to take up land in Fayette and Washington counties more readily than they did in Westmoreland County.[13] While this may have had an effect on the pattern of settlement, other factors such as the paths of migration, the original homes of the settlers and their loyalties, and certainly Westmoreland's exposure to Indian attack during the Revolution contributed to any tendency for settlers to prefer Fayette or Washington counties.

There is little doubt, however, that the confusion over land titles added to the normal burden of the local courts. The county courts of Westmoreland, Washington, and Fayette counties received 654 ejectment cases through 1795—73 percent of which were initiated by the end of 1785. Another 16 percent were begun through 1790, and a final 11 percent through 1795.[14] Thus, the two land systems operating simultaneously in western Pennsylvania added to the confusion and uncertainty of these early years of settlement.

A final factor that greatly disturbed the early years of settlement in western Pennsylvania was the very real fact of war. War in western Pennsylvania antedated the revolutionary conflict by a full year. The continuing pressures of land speculators and settlers led the Shawnee Indians, reacting to, among other things, the reoccupation of Fort Pitt by the Virginia militia, to initiate the conflict known as Dunmore's War. This war also reflected some of the bitter state rivalries associated with the border dispute. The sharp battle that occurred on the banks of the Ohio at Point Pleasant, Virginia, caused the Indians to withdraw into Ohio, which ended the conflict for the time being.

No sooner had these hostilities subsided than troops were recruited for the Revolution. Both Virginia and Pennsylvania regiments were raised in western Pennsylvania and served in the East during 1776–1777. The war brought a renewal of Indian attacks in 1777, and throughout the years of the war, Indian provocations, now with British support, occupied the attention of harried frontiersmen. Recognizing the danger to the exposed frontier, Congress appointed, in mid-1777, the first of a succession of officers to organize frontier defenses from Fort Pitt. Some success was attained by 1779, but thereafter, one defeat followed another. In 1782, the defeat of Col. William Crawford in northern Ohio left the frontiers open to attack. On 13 July, Hannastown, the small settlement of some thiry log cabins that served as the county seat of Westmoreland County, was burned to the ground by Seneca Indians supported by the British. Sporadic attacks continued for several months until after the formal peace treaty in 1783.

Thereafter, the Iroquois and then the Delaware and Wyandot tribes gave up their claims to Pennsylvania. This divided the Indian opposition and removed most of the direct threat to local settlers by transferring it to Kentucky and Ohio. Frontier hostilities returned by the end of the decade and did not end until Gen. Anthony Wayne's victory at Fallen Timbers in 1794 and the resulting Treaty of Greenville. Western Pennsylvanians suffered little after the Revolution, but the fears generated by these Indian conflicts remained in the minds of settlers for many years.[15]

These military troubles taxed the economy of the new frontier region. Trying to supply the needs of war with a frontier economy was most difficult and, indeed, proved impossible. War demanded men, munitions, food, and livestock, but frontier western Pennsylvania as yet had little surplus of any of these. The manpower needs of the war conflicted with the needs of wresting a living from the wilderness.[16] There was to be no munitions industry in the region for another decade or more. Arms were limited to personal side arms and whatever could be brought in by various means, including occasional river forays to New Orleans. Harvests, which as yet yielded little more than the basic needs of the area, were stretched to supply the army, while a late-season drought in 1780 created a flour shortage in spite of a good harvest. A combination of army impressments and worthless currency drove settlers to hide their reserves of livestock in the woods.[17]

The combined impact of these events upon settlement was marked. Large northern and western sections of the region, some of which had been well settled, were sparsely populated—if populated at all—as the Revolution closed. In addition, the war undoubtedly slowed the processes of clearing land and of increasing crop and livestock production. Furthermore, if conditions evident in the 1790s were indicative of what would have occurred during the 1780s except for the traumas of war, then it must be concluded that the whole complex of factors that make for nascent industry, for the development of towns, and for the beginnings of commercial agriculture were also delayed by a decade filled with war and political instability. The passing of these difficulties opened the region to vigorous settlement and growth.

Population Growth

In spite of these many difficulties, the population of western Pennsylvania apparently continued to grow even during the war and clearly increased rapidly following the war. In order to study the population of western Pennsylvania and its rate of growth, as with any region settled before the 1790 census, one must develop estimates of its early population. Fortunately, there are means available for obtaining a fairly accurate estimate of western Pennsylvania's population at the close of the Revolution. Such an estimate can be obtained by using the tax assessments for Washington County (1784) and Westmoreland County (1783) and a ratio of 4.65 persons to 1 taxable person derived from a local census included as part of the Westmoreland return.[18] By using these figures, the white population of Washington County in 1784 has been estimated at 15,900, and the white population of Westmoreland County in 1783 at 17,600, making a total of 33,500 at the close of the Revolution. The number of slaves has been estimated to be 4 percent or more of the white population, so that the total population of western Pennsylvania at the close of the Revolution was approximately 35,000 persons.[19]

By using this estimated population base and the censuses of 1790 and 1800, one can establish a rate of growth for western Pennsylvania and compare it to that of the state as a whole. Such a comparison indicates that the free population of western Pennsylvania increased approximately threefold—from 33,500 to 94,893—during the period between 1783–1784 and 1800, while the population of the state as a whole increased about 40 percent during the decade 1790 to 1800. The percentage of increase, however, was significantly lower in western Pennsylvania during the decade of the 1790s. Whereas it had been 87.3 percent between 1783–1784 and 1790, it was only 50.6 between 1790 and 1800. This compares to a percentage of increase for the state during the 1790s of 39.5, a figure not too much less than that for western Pennsylvania.[20]

By using similar comparisons, but on the basis of the increase in the number of taxables at seven-year intervals—and in one case nine years—it is possible to pinpoint somewhat more accurately when the great population surge took place (table 1.1).[21] (Of course numerous intangible factors—not the least of which is whether wartime tax records are particularly

TABLE 1.1

Average Annual Increase and Percentage of Increase in the Taxable Population, Western Pennsylvania and Pennsylvania, 1770–1800

Taxable Population	*1770–1779*	*1779–1786*	*1786–1793*	*1793–1800*
For Western Pennsylvania				
Average annual increase	541	583	750	500
Percentage of increase	138.7	121.2	61.0	25.3
For Pennsylvania				
Average annual increase	1,657	1,749	3,460	3,173
Percentage of increase	37.5	22.4	36.2	24.4

accurate—make it necessary to interpret these figures as illus-
trative of a general trend rather than as exact measurements
of Pennsylvania's taxable population.) These figures indicate
that the war years did not appreciably slow the population
growth of western Pennsylvania. Following the war, however,
a sharp increase took place, which apparently peaked around
1790 and definitely slowed in the last half of the 1790s. The
normally high percentage of increase shown by any newly
settled area was evident in western Pennsylvania, but then it
declined steadily until, by the end of the century, the rate of
increase for western Pennsylvania was nearly the same as for
the entire state. With western Pennsylvania and the state as a
whole growing at approximately the same rate, the frontier
period in western Pennsylvania had ended.[22]

Another comparison, the ratio of population to taxable
population, also suggests that an end had come to the period
of rapid frontier growth in western Pennsylvania by 1800. By
comparing this ratio for each western Pennsylvania county in
1800 with the ratio of 4.65 to 1 from the early 1780s, it is
obvious that western Pennsylvania had changed (table 1.2). A
combination of fewer absentees, more wives and children,
and more propertyless persons attracted by the economic op-
portunities in the area had markedly increased the ratio of
persons to one taxable. It is important to note that the highest
ratio corresponded to the county with the greatest urban development by 1800—Allegheny County. When compared
with other ratios for Pennsylvania, the ratios existing in western Pennsylvania by 1800 were similar to those for the older,
well-settled regions of the state. For the year 1800, in fact, the
western Pennsylvania ratio was actually slightly higher than
the ratio for the entire state.

In summary, on the basis of these various population figures, it can be stated that western Pennsylvania had a very
sizable population by the Revolution, and that this population
probably continued to grow somewhat, even during the war
years. Certainly, by the end of the war, the population num-
bered in the thirty thousands. In the years following, population increased rapidly, reaching a peak during the early
1790s. In terms of straight numerical growth, the area grew

TABLE 1.2

Ratios of Population to Taxable Population,

Western Pennsylvania and Pennsylvania, 1783–1784 to 1800

Place	Ratio of Population to Taxable Population
Western Pennsylvania, 1783–84	4.65 : 1
Western Pennsylvania, 1800	5.47 : 1
Westmoreland County, 1800	5.2 : 1
Washington County, 1800	5.6 : 1
Fayette County, 1800	5.3 : 1
Allegheny County, 1800	6.0 : 1
Greene County, 1800	5.5 : 1
Pennsylvania, 1800	5.31 : 1

Sources: Samuel Hazard, ed., *Hazard's Register of Pennsylvania* (Philadelphia, 1828–1836), 4 (July 1829), pp. 12–13. All 1800 ratios are based on total population; that of 1783–1784, on free population. For free population in 1800, subtract 0.1 from Westmoreland, Washington, and Greene counties, for a Western Pennsylvania total of 5.44. Samuel Hazard used a 5 : 1 ratio in 1829 to estimate 1828 population on the basis of 1828 taxables. Ibid., p. 13. For other comparable ratios, see: Stella H. Sutherland, in U.S. Bureau of the Census, *Historical Statistics of the United States, Colonial Times to 1957* (Washington, D.C., 1960), p. 743, who uses a 5.8 : 1 ratio. James T. Lemon, in "Household Consumption in Eighteenth Century America and Its Relationship to Production and Trade: The Situation Among Farmers in Southeastern Pennsylvania," *Agricultural History* 41 (January 1967): 61, uses a ratio of 5.5–5.8 : 1.

during the 1790s much as it had for the period between 1783–1784 and 1790. In terms of its rate of growth, however, the 1790s found the region slowing down to a rate of increase comparable to that of the state. Various comparisons of the rates of population increase and the ratio of population to taxable individuals strongly suggest that by 1800, the frontier population of western Pennsylvania had been replaced by a more settled population much like that of older areas of the state. This same general conclusion will become evident in other areas considered throughout this volume. Although it was predominately an agricultural region, its sizeable artisan class, large body of landless persons, nascent industries and developing towns, as well as its stable population, indicated that western Pennsylvania had passed the frontier stage of development by the turn of the century.

Thus, the years from the end of the Revolution through

the 1790s were the crucial, formative years in the transformation of society in western Pennsylvania. Prior to the 1780s, the people had been distracted by many problems. To what extent any one of them slowed progress cannot be determined, but collectively, they seem to have delayed rapid growth and development until after the Revolution. Only then could people give their undivided attention to building a new society in western Pennsylvania. Residing as he did on the western fringe of the region, Thomas Ryerson continued to cope with the disruptions of the past. However, Judge Alexander Addison's testimony of rapid change in the early 1790s, whether politically self-serving or not, was the more accurate description of the progress that had occurred.

2   *The Pattern of Landownership*

FEW MEN personified the forces that transformed the western Pennsylvania frontier more completely than Edward Cook. Born around 1740 in the Cumberland Valley, Cook made the arduous trip west across the mountains from Chambersburg in 1771. He crossed Westmoreland County and settled along the Monongahela River at a location that ultimately placed him just inside Fayette County when it was erected in 1783. Cook was a man of means, and he brought with him a store of goods, opened a mercantile establishment, and before long, added a tavern. In the 1770s, he occasionally was accused before the county courts of running a tippling house, but no formal action was ever taken. He invested his wealth in a sawmill and a gristmill, owned whiskey stills, and registered eight slaves under the Pennsylvania gradual abolition statute.

Cook's economic prominence led to numerous political offices. He served not only as county militia lietuenant, but as a justice of the peace, and as a representative to the state's 1776 constitutional convention. His role as justice of the peace led to service on the county courts, and for many years he served as the presiding judge of the Fayette County Court of Common Pleas and the Court of Quarter Sessions. During the Whiskey Rebellion, he participated as a leader in many of the mass meetings, and he was selected chairman of the Mingo Creek meeting. His home, built in 1776, is often said to have been the first stone house built in the region. By 1796, it was but one of eleven buildings on his 600-acre farm, 150 acres of which were now cleared and in production with the help of at least three slaves he still owned. In time, he also platted a town on his land—at a date later than that covered by this study—which is currently known as Fayette City.[1]

Edward Cook's activities exhibited all the dynamics that rapidly changed western Pennsylvania: wealth, mercantile activity, early industry, commercial agriculture, political prominence, even the founding of a town. All of these, however, rested on the greatest economic resource of the age—land. Cook was one of the region's largest landowners and land jobbers. When he first appeared on the Westmoreland County assessments in 1783, he was credited with 1,500 acres. By 1785, he was credited with only 900 acres in Fayette County, and with 600 by 1796. Cook is typical of that early man of means who arrived in the first wave of settlement, headed toward the river valley, and selected large tracts of good land. He then bought and sold land regularly, generating income for his other economic activities. The land indexes indicate that during his lifetime—he died in 1812—Cook sold forty-nine tracts of land. Edward Cook clearly was not a typical settler, but one of the economic elite. Yet, to understand him as well as to understand the average settler, one must examine the pattern of landownership that developed in western Pennsylvania. That pattern turns out to be a very complex one with a few Edward Cooks, many average yeoman farmers, and a surprisingly large group of landless people.

The Land

The western Pennsylvania landscape presented a rugged challenge to an early settler like Edward Cook. Entry into the area required a long and exhausting trip of several days across the mountains of the Allegheny Front. Travel accounts are unanimous in their descriptions of the difficulties involved.[2] Once the settlers descended the slopes of Chestnut Ridge, they entered the hilly country of the Appalachian Plateau, sculpted into rolling hills and steep valleys by eons of erosion.

> This country of Redstone [Fayette County between Con-
> nellsville and Brownsville] has been compared and I think with
> great propriety to a baskett of Eggs, as it is entirely composed
> of hills of every size mingled with each other—none of them

rugged, but round, tho steep and with every variety from the slope of an egg laid side ways, to the roundness of its larger end and the pointed form of its sharp end—these are neither rugged rocky, or stoney in general, but have the same rich soil to their summits and are never too steep for the plough.[3]

This description, penned by Joshua Gilpin in 1809 as he traveled into the region not far from Edward Cook's homestead to check tenements on lands his family had held in Fayette and Washington counties since the days of the Revolution, picturesquely summarizes the views of many travelers. Rev. John Heckewelder, traveling the Glade Road just a little north of Gilpin's route in 1797, also noted the rugged terrain and its impact on vital water supplies. "This country, however, has many deep valleys and the water gives out early in summer. Consequently, one meets with many tread mills, with which the farmers grind their corn."[4]

Both Gilpin and Heckewelder noted "a very productive soil" and the picturesque quality of settlements splashed across the landscape among large areas of woodland. Heckewelder found "finely situated plantations" but with "much dead timber" still standing in the fields. Gilpin thought the landscape presented a pleasant view "because about as much of the wood has been cleared (perhaps at least one half) as to form the most pleasing proportion—& every hill has its mixture of wood & field."[5]

Modern soil surveys indicate more variety than these two travelers observed. Beyond the mountains, two soil series dominate Fayette County; one forming a V shape with a strip along the foot of the mountains and the other side cutting through the middle of the county, and the second lying within the V and to the west along the river. A third series dominates much of Washington and Greene counties. These generally are silt-loam soils, but within them the quality varies with location from hilltop to slope to bottom land. The alluvial soils of the narrow creek and river floodplains are often wet and subject to flooding. In terms of productivity, the soils of Fayette County are significantly more productive for agriculture, at least in the modern era, than those of Washington and

Green counties. That may not have been as true when virgin soils were turned over two centuries ago. Fayette soils beyond the mountains are also less steep, the rounded end of Gilpin's eggs, while across the river more of the tips of the eggs appear. The Dormont-Culleoka association of soils covers 75 percent of Washington and Green counties, and over half of these soils in Greene and almost a fourth in Washington have slopes of 25 to 50 percent, 32 percent overall. This variety of soils was noted by astute early observers. George Washington complained that soils on his land (near where Gilpin passed) were not equal to his expectation. "Some part indeed is as rich as can be, some other part is but indifferent—the levellest is the coldest and of the meanest quality—that which is most broken is the richest; tho' some of the hills are not of the first quality."[6]

Into this land in the 1770s streamed settlers who imposed their will on the rugged landscape. The forests were cleared to the patterns observed by Heckewelder and Gilpin. The best lands were quickly claimed, but surely all early landholders could find some portion of good land on which to bestow their labor and begin the processes of cultivation. Water was a crucial attraction, and the Monongahela River became the center of settlement. The river did not attract because it had broad fertile floodplains—on the contrary, the flood plains were narrow and the hillsides among the most steep in the region. So too with some of the creeks that cut their way to the river. The creeks and rivers were sought for transportation and power, vital to the region's development. When summer dried many streams to a trickle, the largest and most steady streams had great advantage for the settler located on them. Even so, river traffic often was impossible in dry seasons, and mills ran out of water, as Heckewelder noted.

As settlers spread over the land, they did so in a distribution pattern that was not uniform. Acreages varied widely, and many people apparently could not purchase any land at all. At the earliest date for which one can determine it—the 1780s—landownership was denied to more than one-third of the population. During the next decade, the percentage of those who could afford to own land continued to decline. In some townships, the number of landless persons climbed to 60 percent; in others there were not more than 10 to 20 percent landless. The size of landholdings was also quite diverse. The average landholder in the 1780s had 200 acres, but a few people had more than 2,000 acres. By the mid-1790s, land sizes generally had declined substantially, and a new form of landownership—town lots—entered the picture. The typical settler, the median taxable individual, owned only 100 acres in the 1780s. By the 1790s, he held only fifty acres, and in one county he was landless.

Geography can best explain the diversity found in the percentages of landownership and in land sizes. It was the townships along the river—with only a few exceptions—that had the lowest percentages of landownership and the smallest acreages. The interior townships in the middle of the counties tended to be next, followed by the eastern mountain and western border townships, which had the greatest percentages of landowners and the largest acreages. The early attraction of the river, the subsequent duration of time, and the intensity with which a township had undergone settlement were the important variables in shaping the early land patterns in western Pennsylvania.[7]

Land Patterns of the 1780s

At the close of the Revolution, western Pennsylvania had more than 7,200 taxable persons, 62 percent of whom were landowners. However, the pattern of ownership varied from township to township and county to county. In general, Fayette County and the river townships had the lowest percentages, while Washington County and the border townships had the highest percentages (tables 2.1, 2.2). The two eastern counties of Westmoreland and Fayette had an advantage over the western county of Washington since they were entered first by the advancing pioneers. Fayette County, in particular, had advantages not shared by the other two. All of the earliest settlements, except for Fort Pitt and Fort Ligonier, were in Fayette County. This area did not suffer from Indian attack

TABLE 2.1
Taxable Population and Landowners, by County and Region,
Western Pennsylvania, 1783–1796

County/Region	Taxable Population		Landowners		Landowners as Percentage of Taxable Population	
	1780s	1790s	1780s	1790s	1780s	1790s
Fayette	1,602	2,473	815	1,158	50.9	46.8
Westmoreland	2,256		1,376		61.0	
Washington	3,418	4,969	2,323	3,232	68.0	65.0
TOTAL	7,276	7,442	4,514	4,390	62.0	59.0
River	2,837	2,692	1,523	1,395	53.7	51.8
Interior	2,901	2,762	1,748	1,590	60.3	57.6
Border	1,538	1,988	1,243	1,405	80.8	70.7
TOTAL	7,276	7,442	4,514	4,390	62.0	59.0

because it was always protected by settlements in Westmoreland to the north and Washington to the west. Furthermore, since Fayette was the smallest of the three counties, and approximately the eastern half of its land is mountainous, settlement was forced into a smaller, more concentrated area, which perhaps stimulated greater interdependence and development. In fact, in the other two counties, the areas most likely to have statistical patterns similar to Fayette County are those contiguous to it.[8]

Because the Monongahela River formed the focal point for settlement in western Pennsylvania, the percentages of landownership were lowest in the townships bordering the river in all counties. From the river, spreading both eastward and westward, the percentage of landownership increased steadily. The majority of persons in the river townships in Fayette and Westmoreland counties were landless, and in Fayette County there was already a majority of landless persons in the interior townships. In all counties, the border regions were the least settled, the least developed, and had the highest percentages of landownership. Within this basic pattern, the eastern side of the river tended to be more developed, be-

TABLE 2.2
Percentage of Landownership, by County and Region,
Western Pennsylvania, 1783–1796

Region	Fayette 1785–1796		Washington 1784–1793		Westmoreland 1783
River	47.6	46.0	59.7	56.5	48.4
Interior	48.8	43.3	68.2	64.7	59.5
Border	68.7	58.6ª	79.1	73.3	94.3
COUNTY TOTAL	50.9	46.8	68.0	65.0	61.0

a. This percentage is somewhat misleading, since it is for Bullskin Township only. There is no data for the 1790s for the largest border township, Wharton, but it was included in the 1780s border percentage. Wharton had no nonmountainous area or town such as Bullskin had in the 1790s, and its inclusion probably would have raised the percentage.

cause settlement came from that direction, and the greatest development occurred in the southeast, because of its protected location.[9] In general, this same pattern held true with regard to the amount of land owned by settlers. The smallest holdings tended to be in Fayette County and in the river townships. Acreages then increased progressively through the interior townships to the border townships, and through Westmoreland to Washington County, with the major exception of Pitt Township (table 2.3).

In specific terms, the full distribution of all 4,500 tracts of land in western Pennsylvania in the early 1780s indicates that the median landholder in all counties held 200 acres of land. In the river townships, the median was a little less, 180 acres, while in the border regions, the median was 300 acres. Mean acreages were somewhat higher, and the modal figures were uniformly 300 acres. In fact, one tract in four was 300 acres, reflecting the newness of the area and the 300-acre-maximum holding designated by Pennsylvania law until 1784.

This distribution also reveals that over 90 percent of all landowners held tracts of 400 acres or less, (table 2.4). Very large holdings were rare and probably most were speculative. Only thirty-four tracts—less than 1 percent—exceeded 1,000 acres and only five exceeded 2,000 acres. At the other end of the scale, 10 percent of the landowners had 70 acres or less,

TABLE 2.3
Median and Mean Landholdings by County and Region,
Western Pennsylvania, 1783–1796

County/Region	Median Acreage		Mean Acreage	
	1780s	1790s	1780s	1790s
Fayette	200	131	209	177
Westmoreland	200	—	240	—
Washington	200	140	241	193
All Western Pennsylvania	200	140	235	189
River	180	123	208	159
Interior	200	118	206	160
Border	300	150	309	251
All Western Pennsylvania	200	140	235	189

TABLE 2.4
Acreage by Decile,
Fayette, Westmoreland, and Washington Counties, 1783–1785

Decile	Fayette	Westmoreland	Washington	Western Pennsylvania
1	1–50	1–100	1–70	1–70
2	50–100	100	70–100	70–100
3	100	100–150	100–110	100–130
4	100–150	150–200	110–150	130–150
5	150–200	200	150–200	150–200
6	200	200–300	200–250	200–250
7	200–300	300	250–300	250–300
8	300	300	300	300
9	300–320	300	300–400	300–400
10	320–2,200	300–1,500	400–4,700	400–4,700

and approximately one in three had less than 150 acres. Collectively, the landowners in the top decile controlled approximately 25 percent of the land, while those in the bottom decile owned approximately 2 percent of the land (table 2.5). To be sure, this was a significant difference, but it was not unusual for newly settled areas, and it was less concentration than existed a decade later. Many large landholdings concentrated

TABLE 2.5
Percentage of Total Land Owned
by Top and Bottom Deciles of Landowners,
Fayette, Washington, and Westmoreland Counties, 1783–1796

County	Top Decile		Bottom Decile	
	1780s	1790s	1780s	1790s
Fayette	25.7	32.9	1.7	0.02
Washington	27.7	36.8	2.0	0.98
Westmoreland	24.4	—	2.2	—

in the hands of a few was not a particular problem in the 1780s.[10]

Certain exceptions to the general pattern are worthy of brief mention. Two border townships, Donegal in Westmoreland and Bullskin in Fayette, had smaller figures than might have been expected. Both, in spite of their mountainous terrain, had small clusters of compact settlement that altered their expected pattern. The Donegal settlement clustered around Fort Ligonier and stretched southward along the narrow Ligonier Valley. There were only sixty-one taxable individuals in the township, and most were small landowners. The western tip of Bullskin Township extended beyond the mountains and contained most of its early settlers. Here, the ford crossing the Youghiogheny River, known as Stewart's Crossing, was one of the earliest points of settlement and later became the site of a town. As a result of these rather intensive settlements, the largely mountainous townships had smaller landholdings than other border townships.

The reverse held true for Pitt Township. This river township had considerably larger acreages than other river townships. Although the township included the little settlement of Pittsburgh, its taxable population was rather small, and nearly half of them were landless. This probably reflects the early economic activity of the town, for the township itself was large and could accommodate many more landowners. The landowners in the township, however, tended to have large holdings. The strategic location of the township had attracted

speculators, many of them connected with the military or Indian trade at Fort Pitt. A number of these holdings still remained and caused the significantly larger acreage figures in
Pitt Township.

Concentrating only on landowners, however, obscures the
true picture of western Pennsylvania, because 38 percent of
the taxable population is excluded. The whole taxable population is better represented by the median taxable person. This
typical settler was not the 200-acre median landowner, but
rather a 100-acre landowner (table 2.6).

The overall pattern for median taxable persons followed
closely the patterns established for landownership and the size
of landholdings. They had larger acreages in the border regions and smaller ones in the river townships. There are even
clearer distinctions between river and interior townships than
exist when only landowners are considered. As a result, these
median taxable persons represented a good cross section of the
class structure of western Pennsylvania as it existed in the
1780s, and associating names and contexts to the numbers can
elucidate the general status of the typical settler. Among the
median taxable persons are a speculator, a single freeman,
several farmers of various degrees of wealth, a widow, and
several landless persons. Table 2.7 illustrates the status of the
median taxable persons for Westmoreland County in 1783.[11]

The lands owned by the median taxable persons in Arm-
strong and Fairfield were typical of the many claiming a tract

TABLE 2.6
Acreage of Median Taxable Person, County by Region,
Western Pennsylvania, 1783–1796

Region	Fayette 1785	Fayette 1796	Westmoreland 1783	Washington 1784	Washington 1793	Western Pennsylvania 1780s	Western Pennsylvania 1790s
River	0	0	0	80	50	50	1L
Interior	0	0	100	100	59	100	40
Border	135	2L	300	200	100	300	100
Whole county/All Western Pennsylvania	20	0	100	100	80	100	50

Note: L = town lot.

TABLE 2.7

Median Taxpayers, Landholdings, and Livestock, by Township,
Westmoreland County, 1783

Township/Median Taxable Person	Acreage	Livestock		
		Horses	Cattle	Sheep
Armstrong				
John Daily	1 tract	—	—	—
Derry				
Andrew Willis	150 acres	0	0	0
Donegal				
Philip Byers	100 acres	1	0	0
Fairfield				
Charles Griffin	1 tract	—	—	—
John Hanna	1 tract	—	—	—
Franklin[a]				
Thomas Measure	50 acres	2	2	2
Hempfield				
William Vandike	100 acres	1	1	5
James Walker	100 acres	1	3	0
Huntington				
Robert Brown	50 acres	3	3	4
James Caruthers	50 acres	2	3	3
Menallen[a]				
William Jolliffe[b]				
Abraham Jackson[b]				
Mt. Pleasant				
William Inman	40 acres	1	0	0
Pitt				
Hugh O'Hara	10 acres	2	2	0
Widow McElroy	10 acres	0	2	0
Rostraver				
William Vance	0	1	1	2
John Worley	0	2	2	2
Springhill[a]				
George Wade	0	2	3	4
Windman Wade, single free-man[c]	—	—	—	—
Tyrone[d]				
William Smith, single freeman	0	0	0	0
Henry Thompson	0	0	0	0

Note: The following returns also included a census figure: Thomas Measure, 6; William Vance, 6; John Worley, 4; William Smith, 1; Henry Thompson, 5.

a. Townships that became part of Fayette County in 1784.
b. No property returned, only a list of names.
c. The entry for Windman Wade was simply "gone."
d. Township became part of Fayette County in 1785.

of land of unknown size in these two northern border townships. These listings had no livestock, and the land probably represents land claims, but not actual settlements. By contrast, the two median taxable individuals in the river township of Rostraver (Edward Cook's township in 1783) were both supporting families without owning land. They were probably agricultural laborers or perhaps artisans who resided on the land of someone else as renters or tenants. The term *inmate* was sometimes given to such people. Windman Wade of Springhill was a young man who had already found little opportunity in continuing to live with his landless parents and took off to seek a better life elsewhere. The amount of livestock owned by these settlers was quite typical of the region as a whole. Few people had more than a few head.

In terms of the actual status of western Pennsylvania settlers, what did these various acreage figures mean? The median landowner held 200 acres; the median taxable person held 100 acres. These were adequate acreages if they had been well cleared, but if most of the land was still forest, then most western Pennsylvania settlers in the 1780s were living at a subsistence level. This appears to be the case.

Only one assessment for the 1780s included cleared land, and that one was apparently inadvertent. Springhill Township in 1783, then a large Westmoreland County township, apparently reported the number of cleared acres, not total acres, in the township.[12]

The median cleared acreage in Springhill was only 20 acres, suggesting that roughly 10 percent of a median 200-acre holding had been cleared. More broadly, when the landless are included, the cleared acreage per taxable person in Springhill was only 12 acres available to support an average family. Some studies have suggested that approximately 40 acres of cleared land were necessary to support an average family on a viable farm. Cleared acreage above that began to allow commercial farming, and above 75 acres cleared allowed definitely profitable commercial farming. Other studies have suggested lesser amounts were adequate for some surplus production.[13] By these standards, western Pennsylvania settlers were overwhelmingly at a subsistence level. It must be added that the amount of livestock in western Pennsylvania was below the levels of older, more established regions. This would considerably reduce the cleared acreage needed for hay, pasture, and grains. Nevertheless, if the figures for Springhill Township in 1783 are at all typical, there was little surplus agricultural production in western Pennsylvania at the close of the Revolution.[14]

The land patterns of the 1780s, therefore, reveal a new, subsistence-level, agricultural society in various stages of development. The river regions had been developed the most; many border regions had scarcely been touched. Most settlers had moderate landholdings, but very few had advanced to commercial farming. A significantly large percentage were landless, making it necessary for small farm clearings to support more than the owner's family. Western Pennsylvania, at the close of the Revolution, clearly had not risen above a subsistence level.

Land Patterns of the 1790s

By the mid-1790s, the land patterns of western Pennsylvania had changed significantly. Confronted by great population growth, the percentage of landownership had declined, and acreage figures were significantly smaller. A few people had been able to concentrate larger holdings, but a new type of property—the town lot—gave rise to a class of smallholders at the other extreme. There was a marked lowering of all median acreage figures, but it was offset by sufficient increases in cleared acreage to allow an important degree of commercial agriculture. Because of the population growth during the decade, a new county—Allegheny—had been erected in 1788 out of Washington and Westmoreland, and another new county—Greene—was to be carved out of southern Washington County in 1796. A number of township divisions had also occurred in response to the growing population. The edge of the frontier had been pushed further west and north, and significant settlements such as Thomas Ryerson's existed in the border regions. These exposed areas were still subject to

Indian raids that were only troubling memories elsewhere in the region due to the uncertain military results in Ohio early in the 1790s. Thus, after a decade of steady growth, western Pennsylvania showed considerably more maturity than it had in the 1780s.

One change in the land patterns from the 1780s was a small decline in the percentage of landownership. (See tables 2.1 and 2.2.) The decline was 3 percent to an overall 59 percent and was about the same in both Fayette and Washington counties.[15] The decline in landownership is also evident in each region, and particularly so in the border townships. These border townships were generally undeveloped in the 1780s, but the impact of continuing settlement had a marked effect upon them. For example, in Smith Township in Washington County, 89.5 percent of the settlers owned land in 1784. By 1793, it had been divided into two townships. The eastern one, still bearing the name Smith, now had a landowning percentage of 70.9, nineteen percentage points lower. The western part of the old township, now called Hanover, had a percentage of 86.0, a figure much closer to the 1784 percentage. This type of graphic change confirms the basic pattern that as new regions became settled their percentage of landownership dropped sharply. This undoubtedly had happened in the river townships and, to a lesser extent, in the interior townships prior to the 1780s. The comparative statistics indicate that this process had now slowed considerably in the river townships by the 1790s, but still showed some life in the interior townships and was very much in evidence in the border regions.[16]

An important new factor affecting the distribution of land in western Pennsylvania in the 1790s was the appearance of town lot owners, the first indications of urbanization. The lot owner with a fourth- or a half-acre lot was a much different property owner than even the small farmer with fifty acres. Persons who owned no other land than their town lots made up 3.7 percent of the landowners in Washington County and 9.5 percent of the landowners in Fayette County. The statistical importance of these people can be illustrated by the simple fact that the overall decline in the percentage of landownership should have been doubled—6.1 percent, not 3 percent—if these lot owners had been landless (table 2.8).

The appearance of town lots had an even greater impact upon the individual townships in which the new towns developed. For example, in Luzerne Township, the overall percentage of landownership increased in the 1790s from 45.6 to 47.9 percent. The reason was not because Luzerne had gained proportionately more landed farmers, but rather because Luzerne now contained the town of Bridgeport in which forty persons—thirty-five of whom owned no other land—now owned town lots. If town lots are excluded entirely from consideration, the Luzerne percentage would have been 41.3 in 1796, or if persons with only town lots are considered landless, the percentage of landownership would have been only 36.7 percent (table 2.9).

The same thing can be illustrated in Bullskin Township where the percentage of all landowners was 58.6 in 1796, but would have been 52.7 if town lot owners are excluded from consideration, or only 46.1 if lot owners are considered land-

TABLE 2.8
Landownership, With and Without Lot Owners,
by County and Region, 1793–1796

County/Region	Taxable Population	Number of Landowners	Percent Landed	Lot Owners	Percentage of Landownership When	
					Lots Excluded[a]	Lots as Landless[b]
Fayette	2,473	1,158	46.8	109	44.4	42.4
Washington	4,969	3,232	65.0	121	64.2	62.6
TOTAL OR OVERALL PERCENTAGE	7,442	4,390	59.0	230	57.7	55.9
River	2,692	1,395	51.8	68	50.6	49.3
Interior	2,762	1,590	57.6	112	55.8	53.5
Border	1,988	1,405	70.7	50	69.9	68.2
TOTAL OR OVERALL PERCENTAGE	7,442	4,390	59.0	230	57.7	55.9

a. Excluding lot owners from both the taxable population and the landed population.
b. Excluding lot owners from the landed population only, thereby increasing the number of landless.

TABLE 2.9
Landownership With and Without Lot Owners,
by Township, 1793–1796

Region/Township	Taxable Population	Number of Landowners	Percent Landed	Lot Owners	Percentage of Landownership When	
					Lots Excluded[a]	Lots as Landless[b]
River						
Luzerne	311	149	47.9	35	41.3	36.7
Springhill	362	136	37.6	17	34.5	32.9
E. Bethlehem	173	108	62.4	9	60.4	57.2
Cumberland	315	164	52.1	7	51.0	49.8
Interior						
Franklin	463	196	42.3	6	41.6	41.0
Georges	281	137	48.8	6	47.6	46.6
Chartiers	241	147	61.0	15	58.4	54.8
Strabane	256	138	54.9	13	51.4	48.8
Canton	156	84	53.8	7	51.7	49.4
Washington	111	80	72.1	65	32.6	13.5
Border						
Bullskin	360	211	58.6	45	52.7	46.1
Greene	341	227	66.6	5	66.1	65.1

a. Excluding lot owners from both the taxable population and the landed population.
b. Excluding lot owners from the landed population only, thereby increasing the number of landless.

less. In the county seat town of Washington, which now had separate township jurisdiction, obviously the greatest impact occurred. From a landownership percentage of 72.1, the percentage falls to 32.6 when lot owners are excluded and to 13.5 when lot owners are considered landless. Furthermore, thirteen of the fifteen people who did own acreage in addition to their town lots owned outlots of small acreage around the town. They were, in fact, still lot owners, the same as those in neighboring Strabane and Canton townships who also owned outlots. None of these people were farmers. Only one man on the Washington assessment owned a large farm. Tavernkeeper John Dodd had 204 acres plus his town lot. The second largest acreage was 56 acres and three lots belonging to the town proprietor, John Hoge. Thus, the appearance of